QMS

Quantum Mass Superstructures

Creating the world you experience

ISBN: 978-1-8383550-1-2

Keekoo Publications

First Published 2012
Revised Edition 2023

Website: keekoo.co.uk

Dedicated to the people of Starlab – past and present

Everyone has part of the puzzle and dreams become reality

Starlab reunion, Barcelona, 2011

Richard Gentle

Richard was born in The White House... no, not that one – in Gloucestershire (UK) in 1961, but has spent most of his life living in Yorkshire. He came into the world with a strong sense of purpose to discover and create.

Inventor, photographer, teacher, and writer – Richard has developed his knowledge and understanding of metaphysics, since childhood. He produced his first booklet in 1987 called, 'How We Perform Negative Miracles,' which was photocopied and stapled together and in 2006, after discovering print-on-demand publishing, he republished the booklet in an updated form.

Always one to keep an open mind for interesting opportunities, Richard contacted blue sky research company Starlab, in 2000, after reading an article in the Sunday Times Magazine, and was personally invited by its founder to work in Brussels, on new technology projects. A year later he was employed by Cranfield University to develop e-learning training modules – used around the world. In 2004, he returned to Yorkshire and joined a small team in Kirklees Council, developing e-learning materials for schools and colleges. 7 years later, he became self-employed as a writer and webmaster. This afforded him the opportunity to focus exclusively on his personal voyage of spiritual and metaphysical discovery, leading to writing more books, which he hopes will be of benefit to others.

Richard has self-published several books, the most popular being: 'Crystal Wand Healing' and 'Seth, Abraham, Bashar! – All that you see is yourself.'

In October 2011, Richard flew to Barcelona for a Starlab reunion where he delivered a talk on Quantum Mass Superstructures – the topic and inspiration for the original version of this book, now in its revised form.

"Anyone who is not shocked by quantum theory has not understood it." – *Niels Bohr*

"Like attracts like, so similar ideas group about each other and you accept those that fit in with your particular "system" of ideas." – *Seth*

Introduction

QMS was first published after a reunion visit to Starlab, Barcelona, on Friday 21 October, 2011. This revised version updates, and adds to, the previous information.

Prior to the reunion, an invitation was sent out requesting talks to be presented to the group. I volunteered and, as time was of the essence, sent the first title that came into my head: Quantum Mass Superstructures.

For three months, I contemplated what Quantum Mass Superstructures (hereafter sometimes abbreviated to QMS) actually meant. Having spontaneously arrived at a title, I now had to follow through with a detailed explanation.

As I pondered on my title, I quickly realised that it made more and more sense. However, the implications were huge and I began to wonder if I had taken on too much for a short presentation. Furthermore, I was short on scientific pedigree, unlike others in the group. Although I had lived and worked at Starlab in Belgium for an amazing few weeks, back in 2000, I was really on the edge of what had been, for many, a way of life lasting a number of years. I did, however, receive an offer of permanent employment – just before Starlab (Brussels) went into liquidation. Starlab in Barcelona still exists, at the time of writing this revision.

After sending a provisional copy of my talk to Starlab, of about 15 minutes length, I re-read the original invitation and it said 30 minutes. In the end, and because a couple of speakers could no longer attend, I actually went a bit over my allocated time.

The turning point came when I tried to find more visual imagery to explain QMS in a way that might be more easily followed by my audience. I discovered that the old 'Tetris'[1] computer game's imagery fulfilled my requirements perfectly.

Mental Connections

Throughout this book, I hope to encourage the reader to think more deeply – whether you are from a scientific, metaphysical, or any other background. I would also like to apologise in advance, to those who suddenly go, "whoa… where's that come from? What's that got to do with anything?" The reason for including some additional thoughts, or slightly obscure information, is because from experience, I know that connections are often made in our minds which are not otherwise made when everything flows seamlessly. It is quite deliberate to throw you off track. It's an example too, of the old adage: 'reading between the lines.'

Where descriptions of science are included, they are on the whole kept basic. This book is an introduction to my theory of the quantum level building blocks of the physical universe, 'Quantum Mass Superstructures' and the ideas that develop from them. It is not intended to supply the physicist with mathematical equations or the mystic with all their answers to spiritual development.

---

[1] Tetris is a puzzle video game created by Soviet software engineer Alexey Pajitnov in 1984.

Contents

Quantum Mass Superstructures 1

The Magus of Strovolos...3

The Sentient Power Field 5

Quantum Mass Superstructures – What Are They?...............................6

    A Little Bit About Quantum Theory 8

Creative Mind...11

Probable Realities...17

The Problem with Truth...21

What Of The Things We See But Do Not Understand? 22

    What If Everything Is Right? 22

    Resonance..29

How Can We Test Reality and Solidify Understanding?.....................35

The Process of Creating..37

    Test 1: Roadworks...38

    Test 2: Vehicles...40

What Role Does Science Have Now? 41

    Why Don't Things Happen As Soon As We Have A Thought About Them? 43

    What Would Happen If Thoughts Became Things Instantly? 44

    Why can't I effect change – as and when I want to?........................47

    Seek and ye shall find...48

    A Failed Thought 48

    Exercising Caution with Empiricism 49

    How Can We Be Sure What We Are Seeing Is Real?......................50

    The Higgs Boson...52

To Summarise...53

    Consciousness and Time...54

    The Spacious Present..54

Finally… 55

Quantum Mass Superstructures

For many years, there have been two camps: the mystical/spiritual and the physical/scientific. What follows, is part of my journey of arriving at a heuristic view to inform further investigations.

Throughout my twenties and thirties, I became very interested in the side of life and existence that we commonly label as "spiritual," "mystical," and "esoteric" – although I now prefer the term, "metaphysical."

Throughout the eighties, I attended many talks and workshops covering subjects that looked at the areas of life experience, not widely recognised, or popular, in a material, deterministic, and empirical world.

People who typically interested me at the time, included: Krishnamurti, Ouspensky, Paramahansa Yogananda, and later, Jane Roberts (Seth).

It somewhat amused me to think that all of the people I was interested in were physically dead by the time I got to hear about them. Eventually, I did catch up with some 'still living' individuals, such as, Matthew Manning and Kyriacos Markides.

However, the only one I actually met and spent any time with in person – out of my developing interest in healing – was Matthew Manning, when I attended one of his weekend healing workshops (circa 1986.)

Over time, I began to formulate my own thoughts and beliefs about the nature of reality and more specifically, my role within it. I wanted to share my views with others but, realised that some of the things I was exploring were quite scientific in nature. However, after sending an article to the New Scientist magazine (under a pseudonym) about where all the dark matter in the universe had gone to, I realised that I wouldn't be taken seriously as a non-scientist outside of the recognised, paper reviewed, scientific community. My article was actually rejected for being too scientific. (I never did understand that.)

It wasn't long before I realised, that if you had ideas about an area of specialism, but you were not a recognised practitioner in the field, then writing a fictional account of your beliefs was by far the best way of testing your ideas on a wider audience.

Likewise, the same goes for people with an interest in science but, perhaps little formal training in physics. Conventional discourse in a scientific community might attract ridicule, whilst writing a fictional story account of your beliefs, for example, Dr Who? or Star Trek, allows you to express your thoughts openly, and detractors can feel unthreatened by your ideas.

For me though, I wanted to know more about the facts. When I first came across Richard Feynman, it was by accident when watching a television programme called 'The Pleasure of Finding Things Out.'

I didn't know anything about him, or that he was a Nobel Physicist but, like many before me, I was captivated by his unique approach to imparting his ideas and discoveries. I read two of his biographical works and also his book, QED: Quantum Electrodynamics – explaining the interaction between light and electrons. I felt camaraderie when I read about his experiments with safe-cracking, as locks had fascinated me as a teenager. In fact, when I undertook my teacher training in 1989, aged 28, I lived in student halls that unfortunately had too many locks with similar keys. Initially, I didn't mind a friend being able to access my room with his key, when I was out, to watch my old black and white television but, when he started to borrow, and not return, other items, I had to take action. After trying a hidden keyhole blanking plate, which he duly managed to get around, I took the lock apart, removed the lever plates and rearranged them in a new order that still allowed my own key to work. Although it kept my friend out, what I hadn't considered was that the cleaner could no longer access my room. So I went and had a key cut for her, to match mine, and so far as I know, this could still be in use to this day.

Of course, there are some scientists who are not keen on mavericks, no matter how brilliant they might be. But, for me, anything that helps to make science interesting and accessible, or dare I suggest entertaining, has to be worth taking notice of.

The Magus of Strovolos

Back in the eighties, I read a book called 'Homage to the Sun' by Kyriacos Markides, who spent time in Greece with an elderly man they called 'Daskalos – The Magus of Strovolos.'

Two things stuck with me for many years. The first was when the Magus healed a woman's spine to cure her backache. He allegedly turned her vertebrae to a spongy consistency, realigned the spine and re-solidified the bone again. At various points in the procedure,

Kyriacos was actively encouraged to feel the woman's spine for his own proof of what was happening.

When questioned, the Magus explained that he used his 'etheric[2] hands' as well as his physical hands to do the procedure. In other words, he worked at a level beyond the apparent physical and employed a unique projection of consciousness.

The second account was an experiment the Magus told Kyriacos about; an experiment to turn a small cube of lead into gold. The Magus explained that he chose lead as being the closest form he could find to gold before he attempted the transition – because he had managed to project his conscious awareness into the lead and the gold to examine the make-up of both. With this knowledge, he then projected back into the lead and rearranged the molecular composition so that it was identical to that of the gold. What surprised him was not that the lead did indeed turn to gold but, that it would not remain as gold and very quickly reverted to its original state of lead.

Now, whatever you may think about the authenticity of the experiment, it is not whether turning lead into gold was possible that got me thinking. More importantly, it was that he said the gold changed back to being lead.

So why is this important? I believe that the reason is, because the lead knew that it was not gold. Therefore, **at a quantum level of existence, everything knows what it inherently is**. You can apply this view to pretty much everything.

---

[2] The etheric body, is sometimes described as the first or lowest layer in the human energy field or aura, and said to be in immediate contact with the physical body to sustain it and connect it with "higher" bodies. In healing, the etheric body is healed first and the physical body, after.

The Sentient Power Field

Many years ago, Eugene Halliday[3] described a "Sentient Power Field" in a booklet he called "Truth."[4] He said that the field was a 'moving, feeling field that permeates the whole universe.' Through the power of creative mind, the resultant stresses on the field make apparent, the physical aspects of the universe that we can experience.

It is quite likely that Albert Einstein[5] had a feeling about the sentient field and attempted to develop it as his [at the time, illusive] "Unified Field Theory."[6] Of course, had he been more accepting of quantum theory at the time, his focus may have revealed another great discovery,[7] rather than just his famous quote: "God does not play dice."[8]

---

[3] Eugene Halliday (1911 to 1987) was a British artist, writer, and teacher. For a large part of his life he lived and taught in Manchester and Altrincham, England, UK.

[4] Truth by Eugene Halliday – International Hermeneutical Society (V) Tan-y-Garth Hall, Llangollen, Clwyd, Wales. (Publication date unknown).

[5] Albert Einstein was a German-born theoretical physicist, widely acknowledged to be one of the greatest and most influential physicists of all time. Einstein described himself as an agnostic.

[6] The UFT term was coined by Albert Einstein, who attempted to unify his general theory of relativity with electromagnetism. The "Theory of Everything."

[7] At some level, he may have prevented himself from achieving such a discovery in order for humanity to first come to terms and experiment with the special theory of relativity.

[8] On one occasion Bohr apparently answered: "Einstein, stop telling God what to do."

Quantum Mass Superstructures – What Are They?

They –
- Originate from creative mind
- Grow through attraction
- Bond by agreement
- Expand through reinforcement
- Solidify over [experienced linear] time

Terminology

Because I am inevitably going to struggle with terminology to illustrate my examples, I have to link to something more familiar. I am also conscious of the fact that some terms already hold well-defined meanings and, for me, this can easily lead to a misunderstanding. For example, I often use the term particle, to denote anything from the smallest element of the universe, right up to any bits of something, even though it has been argued that there are no particles, only different quanta. However, for my examples, it may be wiser to transpose the emotive term 'particle' for 'something.'

Therefore, by example: Two "somethings" form a relationship based on at least one common denominator. It could be as simple as having some awareness that there could be another like itself. The somethings become bonded by agreement on shared commonality or attraction. Other somethings who also share this commonality are attracted to the first two somethings and gradually an expansion of commonality develops into a solid, shared experience of existence – which, like cell division, can grow exponentially – almost becoming a society of collaboration in equilibrium. In fact, one might suggest that the expansion of life through reproduction could be seen as a method to maintain and promote agreement on what exists.

One of the interesting and critical things about any quantum mass superstructure is that, **as awareness and acceptance grows, reality becomes more solid.** The term solid is relative, since it could be a literal form of solid in the physical domain, or it could be non-physical solid, such as a lasting memory.

This was nicely illustrated in sci-fi writer Brian Aldiss's book, 'Cryptozoic.' The story is about a team of people who have developed the ability to mind-travel into different time eras and function in a physically conscious awareness of their environment; those with limited experience tend to arrive in the Jurassic period and those with highly developed skills can go back to more recent past times.

The travellers often witness other time travellers in the same geographical locations but, at slightly different moments of existence, appearing in the form of ghostly presences bleeding through to each other's perceived time locations.

The main character in the story bears witness to a series of events and discovers that on one occasion he is unable to pass through the walls of a very old stone building. It seems that the recognition of the existence of the house through many life times has even made it solid in the experience of the time travellers – so on this occasion, he has to enter through the door in a normal way.

Another significant component of the story is that the building is made from stone. Whether or not any of this was in the mind of Brian Aldiss when writing his story is irrelevant but, it has been helpful in triggering my own thoughts in the area of QMS. Stone is a very long-lasting material; its capacity for change over time is also significantly slower than many other materials. Our ancient civilization ancestors also used stone, both for building and inscription.

A Little Bit About Quantum Theory

It is generally accepted that particles[9] in a quantum universe can apparently exist simultaneously in more than one place and time. It has also been found that quantum particles have a tendency to change in some way when an observer chooses to focus attention on them.[10] For scientists, quantum particles have an annoying and rather cheeky quality about them, in the sense that they won't stay still, or in one place, long enough to be measured or rounded up. Therefore, in a quantum universe, no one can really say that anything is certain or predictable. This results in the word "probability" being included in most sentences relating to quantum outcomes, with comments such as: there is an 'x' level of probability that event 'A' or event 'B' will, or will not, occur. (Seth[11] also has much to say on 'probabilities' in his teachings.)

As an addition to the above, in relation to quantum particles not being easy to control, research is moving towards using the processes of holography.[12] The hope is that quantum particles can be 'bound in place' in a way that makes them practical to use (something more recently adopted in areas of research into 'quantum computing.'[13])

---

[9] Actually, according to Art Hobson, Prof of Physics, Univ. of Arkansas: "There are no particles. Nothing in the universe is made of tiny particles. Everything is made of quanta, which are spatially extended bundles of the energy of various sorts of fields."

[10] Look at Thomas Young's 'double-slit' experiment, which you can find on the Internet.

[11] Op.Cit. Seth and Jane Roberts.

[12] At the time of writing, some interesting research is being undertaken with the view that holography could hold quantum particles in position and this would lead to the possibility of quantum computing being feasible. (One paper already written on this: Quantum computing in a piece of glass – Warner A. Miller, Grigoriy Kreymerman, and Christopher Tison – Department of Physics, Florida Atlantic University.)

[13] A quantum computer is a computer that exploits quantum mechanical phenomena. At small scales, physical matter exhibits properties of both particles and waves, and quantum computing leverages this behaviour using specialized hardware.

This would also link with 'quantum entanglement' and theoretically two holographic quantum 'chips' could communicate with each other through time and space. Put another way, particles can become intertwined so that they always share the same properties, even if they are separated. Also, a change in one particle would be mirrored in the other and this links with some principles of basic quantum [information] teleportation.

As a further comment in this revised edition of QMS, I would state that time and space are actually illusional, so the distance between an entanglement is actually zero, regardless of perceived physical distance between the particle separation. (Read some Jane Roberts' Seth[14] books on this.)

Another recent development is 'Bubble Theory.'[15] Interestingly for me, prior to this theory being proposed, I had already started using the term 'bubble' in my own bubble theory which could explain the contradiction of both a non-physical and physical universe. Metaphysics claims that nothing physical is real, and yet, as humans, we will swear to our graves that our universe is physical and that both personal experience, backed up by science, proves this. But go and ask the scientists at CERN[16] and they will tell you that once you view our universe at the levels of their powerful equipment, nothing appears physically bonded together – everything is in a state of movement. So although something might be physically observed, it shows no static solidity. I therefore proposed that the nature of our

---

[14] In 1963, Jane Roberts began channelling amazing information from a non-physical entity who referred to himself as Seth. This information became broadly known as The Seth Material.

[15] The Bubble Theory arises from the nature of cosmic inflation, which views the universe having expanded exponentially in the first tiny fraction of a second after the Big Bang. In this scenario of the 'multiverse' concept, some parts of space-time expanded faster than others. This created 'bubbles' of space-time.

[16] CERN is the European Organization for Nuclear Research. The name is derived from the acronym for the French Conseil Européen pour la Recherche Nucléaire, or European Council for Nuclear Research, a provisional body founded in 1952 with the mandate of establishing a world-class fundamental physics research organization in Europe.

physical universe resides within a bubble of existence in a dimension of a non-physical universe. You might also compare this with a sort of more advanced dream-like state of existence, where awareness is ordered in a more controlled way for learning and conscious evolution to gain an alternative self-realisation.

The other thing about the quantum universe is that it is constantly changing vibrational energy – vibrating at many different frequencies which determine, among other things, the range of solidity for physical substance. In simplified terms, we can have many radio and television stations, simultaneously existing, without interfering with one another. To access a particular frequency, we 'tune into' it, at which point its information becomes apparent. These invisible frequencies can also pass through us at levels where we are generally, or mostly, unaware and unaffected. If you were able to grab a caveman from our pre-history and place him with yourself, in an open field, and stream a video on your mobile 'smart' phone, this would undoubtedly be magic beyond his comprehension. Popular science fiction would also describe the invisible presence of something apparently sharing the same space, as 'out of phase.' Two radio stations are effectively out of phase with each other, but simultaneously share the same space, in the sense that we can easily tune between them in our current physically experienced moment of now. And scientifically, this is also another thing about quantum particles; their varying ability to share the same space. Indeed, I think it is this property of non-sharing of space that makes water possible.

So far, I have talked about the quantum universe as if it is something that we look at rather than experience. We can in fact illustrate many QMS examples of quantum multiplicity, in our sense of physical reality, in many forms and ways.

We can all experience the duplicity of location when we daydream; you can experience more than one locality at once. Similarly, we now have the means to have multiple, instant, online text or video conversations, with several people in several countries simultaneously at different local times – something we could not have believed possible only a few decades ago.

QMS can be a bit like an assembly line in a factory (though not necessarily in a linear sense.) Lots of separate component parts with a shared commonality, fitting together perfectly to create a larger outcome – something greater than the sum of its parts and managed by conscious creative action.

Let's look at some broad examples of QMS:

- Organised cell structures
- Cultural beliefs
- Social compliance
- Gravity
- Thoughts
- Perceptions of personal reality
- The 'known' universe. In fact, just about everything

Before we continue, we need to talk about the importance of 'creative mind.'

Creative Mind

Let's look at an example of human creative thought and the perception of reality through resulting quantum mass superstructures. I experience something – form an opinion about it – look for evidence that supports my opinion – form a belief – and then either ask others if their belief matches mine, or if I am particularly robust by nature – tell others that my belief should be their belief too.

Eventually, if enough people recognise my belief in their own experience, it becomes solid enough to be experienced by others, not necessarily just in my immediate collective but, among those who perhaps have started to form similar expectations of reality.

Consider now though, a growing collective questioning of a long-held belief that no longer fulfils our need to understand something in the present moment of experienced time. Perhaps something we observed no longer fits the model we have created to explain it.

When I was a teenager, I struggled with maths at school. On one occasion, I remember having to resolve some simultaneous equations. I knew there was a formula I could use but, despite taking notes, I wasn't completely sure I was doing the right things. (These days I'd just look for examples on the Internet.)

In the end, I created a formula that seemed to work – but, only in about 3 or 4 out of 5 cases. It wasn't until I finally received the correct formula that I could get 5 out of 5 correct. So my formula worked quite well for most of the time, even as the wrong formula.

The problem we have as a collective human race is, very often we have become used to something working quite well most of the time and when eventually, someone comes along and asks: "Is it just me, or is something not quite working here?" we have difficulty coping with the idea of change.

The first problem is that once an idea becomes rooted in our physical understanding of our perception of reality, it can be very difficult to remove it – a bit like a deeply held engram.[17]

For a start, it is physically real to us; we therefore know it must exist and it's worked just fine up to now – so why change it?

---

[17] An engram is a little program that [hypothetically] runs in the background and is often not experienced consciously but, which determines our behaviour in certain circumstances. Human engrams often result from a significant positive or negative experience which is unconsciously internalised and remains in a 'running' state, ready to become active when similar circumstances appear to arise again at some future time. A postulated biochemical change that represents a memory.

Secondly, when we do not want to accept something different, we actually focus more energy on the fear of what we do not want to happen and therefore reinforce its inevitability.

Someone once said of politicians, 'If you want candidate one to win, stop hoping candidate two will lose.'

From a spiritual standpoint, Mother Teresa[18] was famously quoted as saying:

"I will never attend an anti-war rally; if you have a peace rally, invite me."

What we must do therefore, is focus more of our intention on the outcomes we would like to happen and less on the outcomes that we fear will happen and, as in the quote above, even having the word 'war' in a title, continues to carry the vibration of war, rather than that of peace. In fact, our media often uses the term, 'fight,' when commentating on something unwanted: The fight against cancer; the fight against oppression, etc. This is actually, not helpful.

So, how does creative thought become quantum mass superstructures?

In Jane Roberts' Seth book, 'The "Unknown" Reality,' Seth talks about consciousness units (CU)[19] and electromagnetic energy (EE) units. The complexity of these is best described by Seth:

---

[18] Mary Teresa Bojaxhiu, MC better known as Mother Teresa, was an Albanian-Indian Catholic nun who, in 1950, founded the Missionaries of Charity.

[19] Seth says: "There are units of consciousness and units of matter. The basic unit of consciousness cannot be broken down and is not physical and is not a particle. It contains within itself innately infinite properties of expansion, development, and organisation; yet within itself always maintains the kernel of its own individuality. Despite whatever organisations it becomes part of, or how it mixes with other such basic units, its own identity is not annihilated. It is aware energy, identified within itself as itself, not "personified" but, "awareized". It is therefore the source of all other kinds of consciousness and the varieties of its activity are infinite. It combines with others of its kind, forming then units of

"The EE units represent the stage of emergence, the threshold point that practically activates the CU's, in your terms."[20]

"The CU's, following that analogy, serve as source points or "holes" through which energy falls into your system, or is attracted to it – and in so doing, forms it. [...] As CU's leave your system, time is broken down. [...] New CU's enter and leave your system constantly, then. Within the system en masse, however, through their great and small organizational structures, the CU's are aware of everything happening – not only on the <u>top</u> of the moment, but within it in <u>all</u> of its probabilities."[21]

"The sources are the CU's themselves. <u>In</u> their own way, and using an <u>analogy</u>, now, in certain respects at least the CU's operate as minute but extremely potent black holes <u>and</u> white holes, as they are presently understood by your physicists."[22]

Seth also says:

"Each unit of consciousness (or CU) intensifies, magnifies its own intents to be – and, you might say, works up from within itself an explosive spark of primal desire that "explodes" into a process that causes physical materialization. It turns into what I have called [an] EE unit, in which case it is embarked upon its own kind of physical experience." And: "Units of consciousness (CU's), transforming themselves into EE units, formed the environment and all of its inhabitants in the same process, in what you might call a circular manner rather than a serial one."[23]

This, to me, would be Seth's explanation for the 'Big Bang' which started our 'bubble' of physical reality. It was consciousness made manifest in physical formations.

---

consciousness. This basic unit is endowed with unpredictability. That very unpredictability allows for infinite patterns and fulfilments."

[20] Seth - The Unknown Reality, Vol 1, Section 2: Session 688 March 6, 1974

[21] Seth - The Unknown Reality, Vol 1, Section 2: Session 688 March 6, 1974

[22] Seth - The Unknown Reality, Section 2: Session 688 March 6, 1974

[23] Dreams, "Evolution" and Value Fulfillment Vol 2, Chapter 8: Session 916, May 14, 1980

Seth indeed has a lot to say about the creation of matter, but this comment ties in with the formation of QMS:

"As inner energy forms more complicated gestalts [...] then inner energy continues its communication with the physical matter that it creates about it. When inner energy desires to construct a more complicated gestalt, then it must telepathically communicate this intent and purpose through the matter which it collects about itself, forming a more complicated inner telepathic pattern first, that can then be filled in with physical matter."[24]

Seth also says:

"[We] form matter in order to operate in three-dimensional reality, develop our abilities and help others. Physical matter is like plastic that we use and mold to our own desire, not like concrete into which our consciousness has been poured. Without realizing it we project our ideas outward to form physical reality. Our bodies are the materialization of what we think we are. We are all creators, then, and this world is our joint creation."[25]

And from the same book chapter:

"In a very real manner, events or objects are actually focal points where highly charged psychic impulses are transformed into something that can be physically perceived: a breakthrough into matter. When such highly charged impulses intersect or coincide, matter is formed."

Even without an acceptance of metaphysics, there is a growing sense among scientists that the properties of the universe are best described not by the laws that govern matter but by the laws that govern information. When you accept that CU's exist, then this statement seems quite reasonable.

In a further statement from Seth, there are some similarities with the description of Eugene Halliday's Sentient Power Field:

[24] Seth - The Early Sessions 3, Session 121, January 13, 1965
[25] Seth – The Seth Material, Chapter 10

"Physical matter makes consciousness effective within three-dimensional reality. As individualized energy approaches your particular field, it expresses itself to the best of its ability within it. As energy approaches, it creates matter, first of all in an almost plastic fashion. But the creation is continuous like a beam or endless series of beams, at first weak as they are far off, then stronger, then weak again as they pass away."[26]

Similarly, I believe the above statement could also apply to 'probabilities', insomuch as: the stronger the focus, the increasing likelihood that a particular outcome will render itself visible. If the focus is removed, or weakened, before a point of manifestation can occur, any physical outcome simply does not materialise.

So, scientifically, this 'energy approaching matter' could be science's 'plasma soup' and the 'endless series of beams' could be the sharper focus of probabilities that result in QMS.

Throughout the past several years, there have been a number of researchers experimenting with 'precognitive behaviour', 'retro-causality,' and 'distant connection.' In the first two cases, these have been investigated quite thoroughly by, among others, scientist and former Starlab researcher, Professor Dick Bierman,[27] who set up a series of tests with [human] subjects who were shown a series of random, computer generated, positive and negative images, and their responses electronically recorded. In virtually all cases, there came a point where subjects emotionally reacted appropriately, microseconds before the different images were shown. They seemed to know which type of image was going to be shown, before it was actually shown.

---

[26] Seth – The Seth Material, Chapter 10

[27] Professor Dick J Bierman currently works at the Department of Psychology, University of Groningen. Dick started his academic career with research in atomic and molecular physics and then became engaged in consciousness research. He currently combines his physics background with his experience with experimental psychology research to formulate and test theories (CIRTS) that assume some form of limited retro-causality and that could possibly account for anomalous phenomena like telepathy.

This happened consistently, no matter the number of consecutive, or changing, image types generated.

In the second case, of distant connection, experiments with lab rats, learning to find their way through a maze, demonstrated – through a second experiment, with an identical maze in another part of the world, with different rats – that the same task could be completed more quickly than was accomplished by the first rats, demonstrating some sort of non-physical connection through space, when information from the first rats was somehow conveyed to the second rats. This could also explain why two people can arrive at the same idea or thought, even though they may never have met; or why some creative artists, writers, and musicians, have occasionally falsely blamed one another for plagiarism of work.

Probable Realities

A quality of a quantum universe is that physicists tend to talk in terms of 'probabilities' quite reminiscent of Seth's comments. If you tie this in with the sentient field, you can see that the number of 'thought' stresses could quite easily produce any variety, or quantity, of outcomes. In our new world, nothing is solid or stationary anymore. Everything can be accepted or rejected in an instant. Everything is possible in relation to the thought energy and emotional 'feeling tones'[28] directed at the field. In fact, you could say:

"Quantum physics dictates that it is theoretically possible to turn on your kitchen tap and have a dragon pop out."[29]

---

[28] Seth – The Nature of Personal reality, Part One: Chapter 1: Session 613, September 11, 1972: "Your feeling-tones are your emotional attitudes toward yourself and life in general, and these generally govern the large areas of experience."

[29] Kannan Jagannathan

In October 2011, there were a number of science-related stories in the press. However, three stood out as examples of our changing view of reality: The speed of light; a continually expanding universe driven by "dark energy;" and the largest astronomical telescope array of all time at Alma in the Chilean Andes – enabling us to see more of our universe. Previously, in 1990, the Hubble Space Telescope was launched and in December 2022, the even more powerful, James Webb Space Telescope, was launched. All are providing scientists with more information and imagery, never before seen.

I'd like to take a take a quick look at light, or perhaps, the speed of light as an expression of reluctance to evolve – in the sense that many people do not like to change an established order, even when new evidence is made available.

In 2007, I reached a point in my understanding of personal reality that threw into question, the nature of all physically experienced phenomena. I speculated that the speed of light may only be a constant in a physical universe, i.e. our collective construct of the physical universe as we know it.

Across the centuries, some people have reportedly been able to instantly project their conscious awareness to other places and gather information, later substantiated by people physically connected to those places. This ability permits a person to be simultaneously in, or aware of, two places. In fact, both the Russians, and the Americans, developed such techniques for covert remote viewing[30] of distant locations, without having to send physical people, or reconnaissance equipment, into a danger zone.

This means that potentially, something non-physical, and faster than light, e.g. consciousness, probably exists outside of our ability to measure it with physical instruments.

---

[30] Physicists Russell Targ and Harold Puthoff, parapsychology researchers at Stanford Research Institute (SRI), are generally credited with coining the term "remote viewing" to distinguish it from the closely related concept of clairvoyance. However, many dismiss the whole topic as pseudoscience.

A report began to emerge in the media in October 2011, that scientists working at the Italian centre, OPERA[31], together with scientists in Switzerland at CERN[32], had discovered that a neutrino fired from one location to the other, travelled faster than light – albeit by a nanoscopic margin.[33] This story is interesting for a number of reasons:

Firstly, it flew in the face of everything we think we knew about the stability of our everyday experience.

Secondly, its implications were so far-reaching, that many of the discoveries made over past centuries, such as Einstein's $E=mc^2$, together with discoveries that could be made in the future, were suddenly under threat of having to be re-evaluated. However, by 2012, evidence of an error with a loose fibre optic cable had been discovered and the discovery was trashed.

Despite this, arriving at the realisation that our "fact" may be incorrect is actually not the disaster we might at first have assumed. Science is constantly increasing its ability to drill down deeper into the fabric of our universe. What has happened is that we have penetrated the skull and have now arrived at the brain. We are working more with vibration than we are with tangible solidity – something the researchers at Switzerland's CERN[34] have appreciated for some time.

Whether we eventually, and officially, discover something faster than the speed of light, or not, does not change the speed of light in our

---

[31] Oscillation Project with Emulsion-tRacking Apparatus. The experiment, launched in 2006, studies the rare oscillation of muon neutrinos into tau neutrinos.

[32] Op.Cit. CERN

[33] Time taken by neutrinos: 0.0024 seconds; Faster than the expected time by: 0.00000006 seconds; Over a distance of: 732Km

[34] European Organization for Nuclear Research, known as CERN (Conseil Européen pour la Recherche NucléaireThe) is an intergovernmental organization that operates the largest particle physics laboratory in the world. Established in 1954, it is based in a north western suburb of Geneva, on the French-Swiss border.

physical universe. Remember, our perception of the physical is only a part of what we experience, what we are, or what anything is. Our personal physical senses have limitations, as do the sensors created by scientists. There are always going to be gaps in human understanding and, interestingly, mass[35] is still considered by many to be a mystery. German physicist, Max Planck (1858-1947) said:

"All matter originates and exists only by virtue of a force which brings the particle of an atom to vibration and holds this most minute solar system of the atom together. We must assume behind this force the existence of a conscious and intelligent mind. This mind is the matrix of all matter."[36]

More recently, scientists connected understanding mass with the Higgs Field, which they described as permeating the whole of reality. However, this did not produce the amount of mass expected.

So far, all of this seems very similar to Eugene Halliday's description of his Sentient Power Field.

However, scientifically, most mass comes from energy. Einstein's equation $E=mc^2$ says we have a lot of energy for a little bit of mass, but when the equation is rearranged as $m=E$ divided by c^2 we can get a lot of mass if there's lots of energy; and mass is packed with energy because of interactions between quarks and gluon fluctuations in a gluon field.

So perhaps we are closer to understanding the scientific view of physical solidity through the formation of mass, but then we might also tie this in to Seth's descriptions of CU's and EE units, in the first formation of matter from creative consciousness.

---

[35] Mass is a fundamental measurement of how much matter an object contains. Weight is a measurement of the gravitational force on an object. It not only depends on the object's mass, but also on its location. Therefore, weight is actually a measure of force.

[36] Das Wesen der Materie [The Nature of Matter], speech at Florence, Italy (1944) (from Archiv zur Geschichte der Max-Planck-Gesellschaft, Abt. Va, Rep. 11 Planck, Nr. 1797)

The Problem with Truth

Our personal perceptions of reality are coloured by our pre-existing experiences and personal beliefs – whether formed scientifically, or not. This makes it very difficult to actually know: what is a "truth?" what really exists, and what does not? It is almost impossible for us to respond to anything without personal bias.

Most of us have had help with making sense of enough reality that we don't go mad. Without help and guidance from someone with a measure of living in, and working with, physical experience, we find that subsequent generations will behave very differently from our own and often at odds with our understanding of what is currently truth – real or unreal.

Furthermore, arriving on the planet amongst people who have already made many discoveries about physical existence saves us all a lot of time 're-inventing the wheel.' The real problems occur when individuals or groups become dogmatic in their approaches to truths and force or coerce the populace to believe in the wrong information to preserve the standing of those originating the false beliefs. Two past examples of this are, the Earth being flat and the sun travelling around it. A lot of time was wasted because of this deviation of evaluation. Ironically, the truth was known by ancient civilizations, long before those in our own recorded history got it wrong.

I have often summed up my feelings about 'truth' in this way:

'In our various societies, truth is only what a majority of people agree upon, at any given time.'

There are many examples, throughout history, where truth has changed and you can probably find many examples on the Internet.

What Of The Things We See But Do Not Understand?

In the early 1970s, Erich von Daniken's film, 'Chariots of the Gods,' was shown to UK audiences. The film generated as much controversy as it did excitement, with its suggestion that alien beings had visited the earth and were possibly responsible for many of the 'difficult to explain' wonders we see produced by ancient civilizations. In one part of the film, von Daniken showed a tribe who had, for the first time, witnessed aeroplanes flying over their island. After a while, the planes stopped flying that route and some years later, when another plane flew over, the crew saw to their astonishment, the tribe had built a replica of one of the plane's they had seen previously and were worshipping it in an attempt to bring back the original planes. Of course, the tribe's plane could not fly, even though it appeared to be quite an accurate facsimile. This is a brilliant example of how we can witness something and not understand fully what we are seeing.

What If Everything Is Right?

When I ask this question, I am actually suggesting that even when we make mistakes or decide that some of our beliefs were not quite right, we are still right in what we were, and are, doing. This is part of our process of assimilation and understanding. If we got all of the answers immediately, we wouldn't need to exist as we do – in human form. We would in fact be "All That Is."[37]

People on spiritual paths have often reached the contradictions of their beliefs when suddenly realising that you have to: do without doing; be without being; see without seeing, and so on. Of course, science hasn't been without its own seeming contradictions and, for a

---

[37] Religiously speaking, God. Spiritually speaking, the Universe.

long time, arguments about the nature of light being waves or particles, was only resolved when the wave-particle theory of light was deemed to be quite acceptable: particles of light can travel in waves. In fact, the nature of quantum particles is that they also often behave in waves.

As I said earlier, it is quite possible that one can have the speed of light as a physical constant whilst still having something underlying that is faster than light – there is no contradiction.

As many of you have heard, the 'observer effect' refers to changes that the act of observation will make on the phenomenon being observed. Usually, we claim this at levels beyond normal physical sight. However, we can also witness the phenomena in our physical perception of immediate reality. A similar notion exists as the basis for Chaos Theory and flapping butterfly wings.[38]

One illustrative example I came across, was checking the pressure in a car tyre; this is difficult to do without letting out some of the air, thus changing the pressure. This effect can be observed in many areas of physics.

When you have a thought about any pre-existing idea, you actually change the nature of what exists… albeit in your own perception of reality. Furthermore, you can use this knowledge to alter what you later perceive.

You probably know the saying: "you'll believe it when you see it." However, metaphysics turns this around and suggests that actually, "you'll see it when you believe it:" the effect of mind on matter; the observer affecting a probable outcome.

---

[38] Chaos theory studies the behaviour of dynamical systems that are highly sensitive to initial conditions, an effect which is popularly referred to as the butterfly effect. Small differences in initial conditions yield widely diverging outcomes for chaotic systems, rendering long-term prediction impossible in general.

One of the few truths that can exist in all actuality is that the only time that really exists to us, as individuals, is whatever we are experiencing in every moment of 'now.' Yes, we can look back and project forward a bit but, in terms of taking action, every moment of now is the only time we really control or exist in.

This was strongly delivered by Seth, throughout the series of books written by Jane Roberts and her husband, Rob, which reached their widest prominence in the 1970s and 80s. Seth's two favourite expressions were: "You create your own reality" and "Your point of power is now."

Hopefully, you have started to understand my ideas leading to the theory of Quantum Mass Superstructures, but perhaps there's still some room for a more graphic explanation.

The following simple Tetris[39] represents our nicely ordered and deterministic, Newtonian Universe, where everything fits, and everything is mechanically determined to be able to exist in harmony without collision. Rules are simple and outcomes are predictable:

This next Tetris represents the quantum universe of probability and uncertainty – where many things appear random and nothing can be guaranteed to fit. In fact, you can see that some external intervention

---

[39] Op.Cit. Tetris

might be required to order things to best advantage. We can create rules but, we cannot easily predict the input or the outcome:

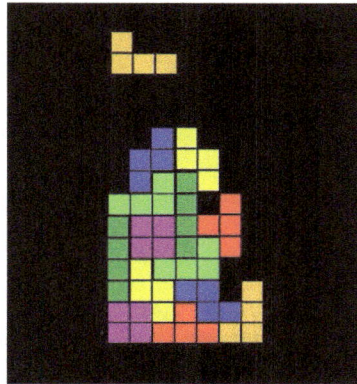

Actually, our quantum universe, until recently, has been more like this. Each of these blocks represents a QMS and these can create further QMS.

For a considerable time, the human race has preserved some sense of perceived order – possibly because a few groups generally controlled the populations of creative thinkers around the world. It was possible for most QMS to coexist – although humans do seem to enjoy fighting each other for acquisition or having wars of righteousness – and this brings us to the touch plane.

When different QMS come into close proximity, there is a likelihood of contact. The point at which contact is made, I have called the "touch plane." The following diagram is simplistic and only for demonstration purposes – in fact, the touch plane is multidimensional and has no obvious shape or line:

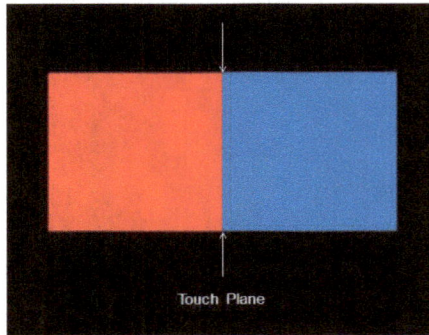

Touch Plane

Below, the light sculpture that I made, illustrates better the nature of the touch plane. Ignore the 'v' shape in the centre and simply focus on the way the colours blend where they touch and begin to merge. This is closer to the subtlety of QMS coming into contact and also shows the effect of the influence of contact.

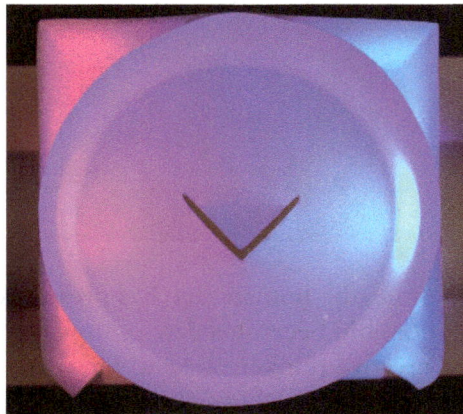

Also notice that the source origin of the two "somethings," here represented by the red and the blue light, are not inherently 'changed;' they still preserve something of their innate identity. However, where they meet, they form a new relationship where influence and/or stress, can occur.

This is a quantum-dimensional view of touch planes and is also representational of human relationships, interactions, and memory:

The main contact is self-evident (where the rings overlap.) However, aspects of each "something" appear in conscious realisation, simultaneously, and in other dimensions of perceived reality. For example, consider the memory of someone who is no longer in your immediate locality. This could be a relative or friend living in another geographical location, or it could be an acquaintance who has died.

Not intended as the Olympic rings but, these next images represent the touch planes of relationships. In the first image, we see a simple two-dimensional representation of associations – so blue knows something of yellow and yellow knows something of black. However, black knows nothing of blue.

In the next image, the same applies but, we can see that whilst red appears to only have association with green, at the end of the line-up, it does in fact have association with blue. This has brought us into a three-dimensional model of association:

This last image is the best I can do to represent a four dimensional association. Red is now linking to blue, green and black:

This arrangement adds another interesting situation. If you consider that the points at which the rings overlap are the only points that share any commonality, the areas where there is no overlap are only known to those parts of the complete rings – perhaps an individual person. Put another way...

Just because green touches red and black, does not mean it can know the aspect of the relationship where red touches black or touches nothing else. One might suggest therefore, that the area of a ring, not in contact with any other ring, represents the private thoughts of that ring or individual. We could go a step further and say that where there is no direct connection or relationship, nothing else exists to that person… and if we go even further: where there is no conscious activity, 'awareised' energy, or stress on the sentient field, we get what appears to be, dark, empty space.

Resonance

Sometimes, we can have a feeling about something which exists, or perhaps we are told or shown something that exists in another person's reality. One example of this, in human terms, might be the knowledge that a famous celebrity exists but, we never actually cross paths. Another example might be knowing that someone loves red shoes but not knowing they eat a lot of cheese. However, someone else may know about their cheese habit and not the shoes… or know about both of those and something more.

If you put all of these associations together to form QMS you eventually create something really big. May I introduce to you, the greatest QMS known to humanity…

The planet Earth:

Let me be clear about this QMS. This, our version of the planet, and the number of QMS forming it, is beyond human comprehension. However, for most of its life, some 4.543 billion years (as we believe its physical age to be) QMS have coexisted in perfect harmony and in such strength of purpose, that we have had to operate within the constructs predefined before our arrival – for example, accepting of everything from the air we breathe to the gravity that holds us down, to the water that we drink.

Our ability to influence perceivable change has been limited by the power and vastness of this planet and the time it has solidified its structures so that they cannot easily be affected by our influence. For much of human existence, as we understand it, we have been able to create more QMS but, nothing that would overwhelm, or not fit with, already existing QMS.

The planet Earth is our most enduring QMS and its formation over a very long time period has enabled it to achieve stability for the safety and well-being of creatively evolving sentient beings, long before we arrived. It gave us a recognisable framework and a position to start from. For a time, the apprentice is not given the means to destroy the work – only the tools and materials required to learn about the work before adding to it.

This has all been going great…until now…

Everything for us, has changed, and one thing that has changed things more than anything, is our use of the world wide web to communicate thoughts, feelings, and ideas, at unprecedented speed and on an unprecedented scale.

Yes, we have come together to create physical cities and engineering masterpieces but, never before have we come together in such large groups to share spontaneous thoughts and have a say to others about our own perceptions of the reality we experience.

There is so much stress now placed on already highly populated areas of the sentient field that it's difficult for everything to fit neatly. We are noticing fractures in our perception, of what we thought was a solid, secure, reality. This is why we now experience, first hand, what it is like to live in a quantum universe.

We now have so many new thoughts and feelings, that it is difficult to create anything lasting or solid. It's all very exciting but, it is causing a great deal of personal and collective insecurity. For the first time in our history, we have realised how much change we can impose on our environment, and we are also realising that we have lost control of our perceived mastery. The apprentice has suddenly found other ways to use matches, beyond lighting the flame on the welding torch.

The interaction of QMS can be very forgiving but, in highly populated areas of the world, we are experiencing the plane edges of colliding QMS in physically manifested feedback and it's where these edges meet that we experience the greatest changes in our perceptions of reality.

I'd like to throw in a thought here that occurred to me a while ago, when a number of programmes about our environmental impact on the planet, were aired on television. One documentary reported on some areas in the oceans where lots of plastic waste seemed to be collecting. I wondered whether this might be forward planning by the planet because, although the Earth is physical, it simultaneously resides in the spacious present, where time and space do not exist, as we understand them. Therefore, it is of particular interest to me that our planet has more sea than land. It's almost as if our future behaviour was already known and provision was set up in a predetermined manner, to mitigate such behaviour when the time, in our experience of physical reality, arrived at this juncture in the Earth's history.

The next image is not intended to be literal, in terms of tectonic plates and earth movement but, it usefully shows in a visual way, how QMS touch planes might react when meeting:

The point is that when QMS touch, something has to change. If the quality of colliding QMS is too different, and smooth blending isn't possible, something new will be created – and in our perception, this may manifest in a number of different ways, appearing as unusual, exciting, or even frightening.

It is possible to alter the course of perceived change but, in the same way that someone who regularly feigns illness as an excuse to not do something may eventually lose control and become genuinely ill, the reality of any perceived situation then becomes more solidified and it seems impossible to reverse the process. A personal core belief[40] may prevent you from changing the reality you experience and also, a focus on what has already manifested takes your attention away from

---

[40] Core Beliefs – generally deeply held beliefs that govern behaviour, regardless of conscious beliefs to the contrary. Closely related to engrams – little programs that run in the background of our unconscious.

seeing in your mind's eye, a different possible manifestation. As previously mentioned, 'seeing when you believe it.' Of course, if you like the environment you are experiencing, it's easier to simply build on having more of the same.

The natural world tends to flow with a quantum universe – blending and adapting in sustainable and co-operative ways:

Creatively aware and thinking human beings quite literally see things differently. By nature, we are uniquely placed to experience self-realisation and have the capacity for creative thought; we can make judgements about our environment and we can impose our will on how we want things to be – mostly.

Lego[41] is another stage on from my Tetris example and is a more accurate portrayal of the way we produce our QMS. As children, we immediately start to try making some sense of our world. The act of building with Lego illustrates this well. Out of a selection of different coloured and shaped building bricks, we experiment with feel, size, appearance, permissible placement, and so on.

---

[41] Lego is a Danish toy production company based in Billund, Denmark. It manufactures Lego-brand toys, consisting mostly of interlocking plastic bricks.

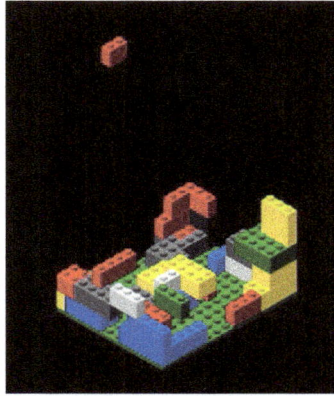

As we get older, we start to imagine more things in our minds that we want to produce in our physical reality. Our ability to arrange and manipulate the Lego bricks becomes more refined and ordered. We know how the bricks work and what we can expect of them. We bring order out of chaos – recognisable structures out of the heaps of building blocks. We can even connect with other creations built from Lego by other creative beings – eventually building many *super* structures and cementing a collective sense of physical reality.

Many people live in densely populated areas, for example, in high-rise accommodation blocks or cities. Furthermore, people in broader terms are now connected through the Internet, bringing vast areas of the world's populations into their own personal spaces. With so many creative minds in close proximity, and a range of agendas and abilities in creating their projections of reality, it is inevitable that some confusion will arise. In a sense, we are seeing chaos coming from order – order being the previously and generally accepted way in which our society seemed to function from day to day. We all have to manage potential information overload by improving our personal abilities to filter information and organise it in a way that we don't go mad!

You might still be asking: "What have quantum mass superstructures got to do with me?" Let's recap.

Firstly, you must accept your individual position, in the context of everything else, and know that what you perceive is what you are creating and what you have already created – your current observations are slightly in the past and 'after the event.' As already said, "You'll see it when you believe it." And secondly, what most people do not realise, and often refuse to accept, is that they are already seeing their creations. This reminds me of the well-known saying: "I can't see the wood for the trees." We can be so focused on looking for something, that we do not realise we are already in the middle of it.

How Can We Test Reality and Solidify Understanding?

There are two things to remember about conventional physical reality. One is that much of it was formed before our arrival. The other is that we can learn about what is here and create from it whatever is possible.

We actually have two realities, as human beings living in the physical world. The first reality is that there are things that form a basic structure and context for our survival and understanding. The second is that we create personal experiences of reality that can vary from other people.

In order to develop and progress our personal learning and understanding, we have to create the circumstances that will help us. This might mean that we create conflict to learn about resolution. In creating this scenario, imagine you are a writer for a soap opera on television. You have locations, key characters, and various events. As the creative writer, you can organise these into any arrangement you desire in order to get the most out of the experience. Everything is recorded and then played back to others so that they too can share the experience of your understanding. This can often save time on everyone having to re-learn the same things. Put another way; when you have general agreement among the majority, no one has to re-test the water.

Put a different way: We create the personal circumstances we need for ourselves. However, what usually happens is that we blame everyone else, but ourselves, for what we are experiencing and then tell everyone that this is what life is like. The joke is still on us though, because we also create the people who will respond to us saying "this is what life is like." We actually create the whole scenario, circumstances and retorts, etc.

We now have two problems: The first is that we have to operate within the confines laid down before our physical arrival, into the physical plane; and the second is: we create the personal reality we experience. Surely this is a contradiction. How can we both be at the mercy of a physical world and at the same time responsible for creating it? Perhaps it's because we are part of the whole 'All That Is' consciousness that created everything in the first place and we simply cannot stop 'creating,' even when we are pretending that our experienced world is separate from us.

For centuries, we have been told by ancient peoples, that the world is illusion – or as they say in India, Maya – centred on the fact that we do not experience the environment itself but rather a projection of it, created by ourselves. Seth says:

"There is no basic difference you see between a hallucinated object and a so-called physical object, except for the number of persons who perceive them."[42]

This is not an easy concept to get your head around. It is also touched upon by Niels Bohr's comment:

"Anyone who is not shocked by quantum theory has not understood it."

---

[42] Seth, The Early Sessions 6, Session 266, June 9, 1966

We might suppose that scientifically speaking, quantum theory is shocking. However, I believe that Bohr's comment was a reflection of his own sudden realisation of the illusion and paradox of physical reality.

Even when we begin to understand this intellectually, we try to do so from our physical standpoint. But the intellect is part of the ego connected to our physical brain's interpretation of limited sensory information. How can you modify your own behaviour to capitalise on what you now know? What you are experiencing is only relative to where your non-physical consciousness has its focus. Einstein talked about the relative position of an observer[43] and Seth has sometimes referred to this as a need for a complete reorientation of understanding.

The Process of Creating

Physically, we can make manifest pretty much anything that we can focus on. This is probably the simplest statement I can make and yet, at the same time, the most complex suggestion for people to comprehend.

I have personally run a series of tests on this idea of creating reality and had some positive results by way of feedback. However, I am not sure that you would rate my methods as particularly scientific or indeed, verifiable after the events. I'll just mention what I did, the results that I observed, and offer you an invitation to experiment with your own similar tests. The other thing I would mention is that I decided to run these following experiments from the position of driving my car. The reasons for this were twofold: Firstly, I noticed that my state when driving tended to be physically relaxed, but

---

[43] Einstein's revelation was that observers in relative motion experience time differently: it's perfectly possible for two events to happen simultaneously from the perspective of one observer, yet happen at different times from the perspective of the other. And both observers would be right.

mentally alert; and secondly, most things that happened as a response to my thoughts, were quickly apparent when driving. That is to say: I had a thought about a road situation and very quickly received feedback which I could directly relate to the emotional thoughts and feelings I was projecting, just prior to the witnessed feedback.

Test 1: Roadworks

I found that my route to work was becoming constantly blocked by temporary roadworks, no matter which variation of route I tried to take.

The more annoyed I became about this, the more roadworks seemed to spring up. All instances of roadworks also had temporary traffic lights.

One day, I decided to be more conscious of what was happening. I drove my route and soon came across the roadworks; their lights just in front of the turning I could have taken – had they been a bit further down the road.

The next day, I decided that I wasn't going to get upset by the roadworks and it didn't matter if the lights were there or not. I drove the route and was about to approach the lights when I noticed that they were now just below my turning and I could proceed uninhibited.

Over the following few days, the roadworks seemed to change position, in relation to my concern about them. When I was feeling affected by them, they would impede my route; when I was accepting of them and genuinely not bothered, my route would be clear.

One day, as I drove down a hill on the way to where the roadworks had been, I came across a new set. This time I could see that workmen had dug a long and deep trench, ready to lay some pipes. I could clearly see that the new roadworks would be there for at least a week.

The next day, I decided to accept the roadworks and this time, rather than cursing them, I would simply enjoy looking at all the different machines being used and generally check on the progress. As I drove down the hill, prepared to stop at any moment, I found to my utter surprise that the roadworks had gone! The trench had been filled and a new tarmac pavement had been laid in its place.

The next day, on my way back home, I came across traffic lights by the new pavement. I couldn't believe what I saw; a workman was digging a hole through the new tarmac. I had to wait for the lights to change before I could proceed.

The next day, in anticipation of the roadworks, I drove down the hill, knowing that I would be impeded but, at the same time, not actually bothered that this would happen. To my amazement, the roadworks had gone and in the pavement was a neatly placed bollard.

A few weeks later, roadworks appeared outside my house. It was the weekend and I was expecting a friend to visit. I had to go to town and on my return saw that signs had been placed, indicating that the road was closed to through-traffic. This was a disaster! I'd arranged that my friend would visit in the afternoon and if she saw the road was closed, she might turn around and go back – and now it was too late to contact her to say that the road wasn't actually closed to my house.

The next time I looked out of the window, just before my friend was expected, the roadworks had gone.

About a month later, on returning from work, I suddenly found a temporary fence blocking the turn into my drive. The road can be very busy and because my turn into the drive is just before a turning into another road, other drivers often do not expect me to turn before the road. This is why the slowing and turning has to be completed quite quickly so that I do not get a vehicle crashing into the back of me. I couldn't believe the stupidity of the placement of temporary fencing:

39

After making an inquiry, I was informed that workmen were repairing a drain and work would be completed the following day. I hadn't been aware of that particular drain causing any problems. I was also wondering what I had done to create these roadworks. Some part of me must still be bothered and still feel as if I am being blocked – or perhaps a part of me wants to be prevented from getting to my work destination. The work remained incomplete for another 3 days.

Test 2: Vehicles

I could be the only car on a stretch of road, and someone would turn out just ahead of me, instead of waiting for me to pass – leaving the road completely clear of other traffic. The vehicle, then in front of me, would immediately impede my previous progress, because they hadn't managed to get up to speed, and would then drive slower than the permissible legal road limit.

This seemed to happen so often, that I began to wonder if it was, in some way, of my own making. The first clue was in my immediate behaviour. The more irritated I became, the more this happened. Over a period of a couple of weeks, I worked at changing my default reaction. I stopped worrying when vehicles blocked my path, and it wasn't long before I noticed a change. Vehicles would take the next turn off the road, or even appear at junctions just after I had passed them, rather than appearing just before I arrived.

A series of further experiments where I either concerned myself, or not, resulted in strong evidence that I was affecting the reality I was experiencing.

I once again reflected on my state of being when driving. I tended to be in a partial alpha state of brain activity and at the same time in a heightened state of concentration. Driving is possibly one of the few times in my daily life when I am completely focused on what I am doing. As I drive, I can often predict the actions of other drivers before they happen and even know if a driver is going to turn off the road, quite some time ahead of when one might register other subtle clues without realising. I'm sure that many other drivers experience this, but perhaps haven't given it much thought.

Now, I know that some of you reading this will be quick to dismiss these results for all sorts of reasons, whether seemingly illogical, unscientific, or otherwise. But, until you have devised your own experiments in this area and examined your own results, it's going to be difficult for me to persuade you that you do indeed affect your reality on a moment to moment basis. Furthermore, if you only look to the left, you aren't going to see anything on the right. You have to be open-minded to the possibility of something, even if it requires you to suspend normal rational behaviour.

I would only ask that if you criticise my writing, you do so from what you know from *actual personal* experience and not from what you have read, or others have told you – no matter how much status you put on their credentials. You have your own mind – use it.

Get a sense of feeling what resonates with you. We all have tendencies to accept and reject according to our previous experiences. However, sometimes we get a deep intuitive feeling that something might be different from our usual belief and perception about it. Follow those intuitive feelings and run a few of your own tests. Note down what you observe.

What Role Does Science Have Now?

Metaphysically, knowing that we are all co-creators of what we perceive, we can create more things, and understanding the process behind our perception of how, and what we create, can speed up our results – ideally producing more of our desired outcomes.

Scientifically, just because the spiritual person can manifest a cup of coffee, does not mean that he/she/they know how it happens.

As creative and enquiring entities, it is not always enough to watch the magician pull a rabbit from a hat – we still want to know: "How does that rabbit appear? How did it get in the hat in the first place?"

If we did not have science to manipulate, test, and explore, physical reality in repeatable and understandable ways on our behalf, we could not have evolved into the quantum mass superstructure we have now become. However, we must remember that, just because someone wears a lab coat occasionally, it does not make him/her/them an authority on all things.

Once, during one of his many public talks, spiritual teacher Ram Dass[44] was discussing sources people considered were reliable knowledge of the unknown and séances were mentioned. Ram Dass jokingly pointed out that, just because someone is dead, does not suddenly imbue them with knowledge and wisdom they did not possess when alive.

There are many examples where people have been encouraged to give over their personal power to others. One example is health: letting a doctor take the greater share of responsibility over your wellbeing. Another example is giving your children to childcare services, so you can go to work. All these may seem quite legitimate and acceptable, but you have so much more power at your disposal to create a more balanced and co-creative, and co-operative approach to your life, once you begin to understand the mechanisms, so-to-speak, behind the physical world facing you. Everyone can potentially gain a good work-life balance.

---

[44] Ram Dass (1931-2019), also known as Baba Ram Dass, was an American spiritual teacher, guru of modern yoga, psychologist, and writer.

Over only a few decades, westerners have become something of a divided society: half believe everything they are told; and half don't believe anything they are told. I would suggest that this, in part at least, is due to the way media reporting has tried to adopt a view of equal impartiality. However, by giving both sides of an opinion, in a 'yes' or 'no' manner, means people have generally taken one side or the other, without exploring more deeply. It's like tossing a coin 100 times: Statistically, you will get close to 50% heads and 50% tails.[45]

As a result, we make many judgements from our confusion, on those who think, or behave differently to us, and we give kudos to those displaying status, celebrity, or popularity, over and above our own feelings, or abilities, to research something for ourselves. Perhaps we don't have time to look into something; perhaps we aren't interested; perhaps we've decided it doesn't have relevance in our own experience. After all, we can't be interested in everything.

Why Don't Things Happen As Soon As We Have A Thought About Them?

How do you know that nothing happens?

Everything throughout the universe is inextricably linked. Metaphysics has always believed this, and science is now beginning to prove it.

As soon as you have a thought about something, you begin a process that may evolve into something greater. You have put a stress on the sentient field. Even when you sleep, your mind continues to work on problems – very often leading to new insights or solutions upon waking.

---

[45] An evenly balanced coin, with a perfectly repeatable flip, has 2 possible outcomes because it only has two sides (heads or tails). This means that the probability of landing on heads is 1/2. So, the probability of landing on heads is (1/2) x 100, which is 50%.

What Would Happen If Thoughts Became Things Instantly?

To some extent, many of our thoughts are becoming instant things all of the time, and the nature of what we experience changes constantly – it's just changing with such microscopic complexity, that we rarely notice. It's like trying to watch a sprouting plant; its motion is slow and gradual. When you look around at your environment, you are, in a way, looking at the past. This is what has been manifested, up to now. It's important to recognise this when you consciously wish to change something in your life. Until you make an inner change, you won't experience a different outer change. All of this can be quite subtle, but as you begin to understand more deeply, the processes behind physical manifestation, you will find that you can gain more by way of preferred physical feedback and conversely, also understand the origins for the less desirable outcomes.

For most of us, instant manifestation for many things would become problematic, since few people have the capacity to think about anything with the exclusion of other interfering and distracting thoughts. Indeed, Seth has mentioned that much of our real work is mental and of the psyche. Most of us therefore, in the normal scheme of things, are given physical time to consider our wishes; time to run through different scenarios before selecting our true desires; and each time we like or dislike something, it firms up what we really want to experience, until a perfectly mirrored manifestation occurs in our experience.

Another reason that many people do not instantly manifest their preferred desires is because they sabotage constructive thoughts through reflective doubt; feelings of personal unworthiness; and any number of other cross currents of resistance to desired outcomes. Furthermore, a strong desire or need is initially required, followed by an imagined outcome, strong expectation of success, but no attachment to end results.

Remember also, that in many cases, we are trying to effect a change on something that has already formed a solid reality in our perception and we are attempting to change this solidity – in the same way that the Magus of Strovolos claimed to change the solidity of bone. But in his case, he was able to see the situation differently, with a clarity of focus, and apply knowledgeable practice that supported his expectation for a desired outcome. This is possibly the single most important thing to understand about QMS: You do not change solidity by pushing against it – you change solidity by seeing it differently, within yourself.

Instant manifestation often occurs when:

- A fleeting thought is in perfect harmony with a deeply held desire, or is in alignment with one's true self (sometimes at an unconscious level of awareness)
- A time of extreme stress focuses the attention to the exclusion of all other stimuli: facing death; an urgent need for something; or an inability to see clarity in confusion
- A moment of clarity appears at a time when we feel at peace, or have great love and acceptance for something
- A group of people focus intently on one objective
- We 'surrender' to the non-physical to help us in the physical world

Remember: Instant creative manifestation is a direct by-product of sharp mental focus on the sentient field. At the same time, can we see in our mind's eye, something different to what we appear to perceive in our sense of current reality? This could be one of the reasons why most people are encouraged to close their eyes when meditating. It's not easy to imagine something different when you are consciously receiving visual stimuli of a reality you want to change.

It is very easy to become confused by physical reality. Much of science is confused by it. The problem is that we are working with only the reality we can experience with the physical senses and physical tools, we have available to us. Metaphysically, we experience the reality that we have created on individual levels. Also, from a metaphysical perspective, everyone resides on their own version of the Earth. Seth tells us, we each have our own individual physical reality, and that we don't actually share physical time and space with another, because we're in our own dimension of existence; that our reality is re-created continually from the spacious present, and that re-creation is what we translate into, what to us seems to be, movement or motion. It's amazing we can agree on, or collaborate with, anything!

I once asked a friend how we could both go into a room separately, one or either of us never having been in that room before, and in a later discussion agree on the nature and appearance of graffiti on the walls? At the time, no satisfactory answer seemed forthcoming. A year later, I was watching a film with others – none of us ever having seen the film before. I wondered: "If I create my own reality, how can anyone else agree that they are watching the same film as me?" Finally, my friend gave me this answer: You create your own reality.

"Yes," I protested, "I know that!"

"No," he said. "You create your own reality!"

Suddenly, I realised what he meant. I create *every part* of my own reality, including the part where I can watch the same film with other people and they can agree with me that we are seeing the same film. (Seth would say that we constantly send out telepathic information between each other and this enables us to share elements of agreed reality).

The implications of this are, as Spock from Star Trek would say, "most interesting." This means that I have personally created the environment I need to progress my life path, tailored perfectly to me, my needs and desires. If you multiply this to every human being on the planet – what an amazing situation! And because many of us want to experience similar things, we form conscious collectives with others and, where required, come together to share specific situations and experiences. This creates an incredibly complex multidimensional tapestry of possibility. It also allows us as individuals to work through all the aspects of our nature that we wish to develop, change, improve, etc.

I have often jokingly said to friends, that possibly I and only a few people in my immediate reality actually exist; everyone and everything else is merely padding to help me feel less lonely. Another friend's take on the same feeling was that "Maybe only a few people have souls." Conscious life often seems like a video game where reality fills in the gaps as we turn our heads, or move around our environment. Most of the people we see, we don't engage with, while others play a small role in our day, like walk-on film extras.

Why can't I effect change – as and when I want to?

The short answer to this is that you live as a product of the quantum mass superstructures that you believe are your reality in the physical world. This situation is so strong, that few of us can even change our regular behaviour in our dreams.

Some people can 'lucid' dream – consciously influence the dream within the dream state. In this situation, sometimes you feel constrained to take action in dreams that, on waking, you cannot understand why you did not act. Until that is, you realise that your beliefs in physical reality are constraining your freedom in the alternative realm.

The best creators – those who manifest a change – are able to:

- Focus the mind with clarity – excluding all other distractions
- Emotionally experience the outcome before it has happened

- Know without doubt that what they expect will come to pass
- Express genuine gratitude for *any* outcome resulting from their focus

This is an expression many of you will be familiar with:

Seek and ye shall find

Somebody, who understood the process of creation, left this message. Unfortunately, the full explanation was either mostly lost, or not possible to give in an understandable way. Essentially, as we look for something, we stimulate conscious energy that stimulates probabilities for finding it and materialising it in our experience.

A Failed Thought

Many of us get very close to manifesting something, only to give up or become distracted by something else. Remember what Eugene Halliday said about the Field. Focus puts stress on the Field to manifest physicality. If the focus is removed the stress is relaxed and the manifestation does not continue – the field collapses back into itself. You can dip your hand into an ocean and extract a handful of dripping water but, when you release it, all you can see again is the ocean.

In my own life, I pack away surplus possessions in boxes and store them out of sight. Eventually, I forget what is in the boxes. I do not miss my possessions and to all intents and purposes they no longer exist. If they are left long enough, they will actually decay – particularly if they are in no one else's reality, probable or otherwise, to keep them in existence. There's actually a touch of 'Schrödinger's cat'[46] in this example.

Exercising Caution with Empiricism

For many years, the world was content to believe in a deterministic, Newtonian, almost mechanical, universe – until the likes of Heisenberg, Bohr and others, recognised what has now become our Quantum Universe with all of its probabilities, at times [apparent] chaos, and new particle naming.

Whether you are a scientist or not, no one should ignore the possibilities a quantum universe has to offer us. We must not limit our thinking or experience by accepting our perceptions of reality as fixed conditions, or axioms. Furthermore, we cannot rely purely on the views of other people and simply represent them verbatim to others, without really having a personal direct experience of our own.

Much of our personal reality is formed in physical dimensions. However, we also have a quality that connects us in other ways to everything in the universe – much of it totally non-physical and timeless in our terms. Occasionally, we tune into these other aspects of ourselves and can indeed utilise them to great personal effect. It is doubtful though, whether we will ever be completely convinced, as a human collective, that our experience is of our own making.

How can we be sure whether, or not, a QMS is representative of an actual truth, or simply imagined through popular hearsay? The short

---

[46] Schrödinger's cat – a hypothetical cat may be considered simultaneously both alive and dead, while it is unobserved in a closed box.

answer is we cannot. All we can really say of truth is this: truth is what enough people believe is right at any given time.

How Can We Be Sure What We Are Seeing Is Real?

This is an age-old philosophical question attracting much debate. On a personal level, I had a friend who, after a stroke, lost the vision in the centre of her eyes – not because the eyes were damaged, but because the brain was damaged. A black area obliterated her view for several months, and she could only see ahead by turning her head slightly sideways. Eventually, the black spots vanished and her vision seemed more normal – until she started to see people and objects disappearing in front of her.

One day she watched a "mad man" walking up the hill opposite her window, gesticulating to the air and talking with heated excitement. As the person approached closer, my friend suddenly saw a second person next to the first – they were in normal, animated conversation.

What her mind had done, was fill in the gaps of what she was physically blind to with what seemed rational – i.e. the surrounding landscape – in order for her brain to make sense of what was being observed through the eyes.

Perhaps the truth for everything is an extrapolation of what Heisenberg said – 'we cannot know with any certainty.'

In a similar vein, surrealist artist, René Magritte once said: *"This is not a pipe."*

Ceci n'est pas une pipe.

Below is a well-known test of perception:

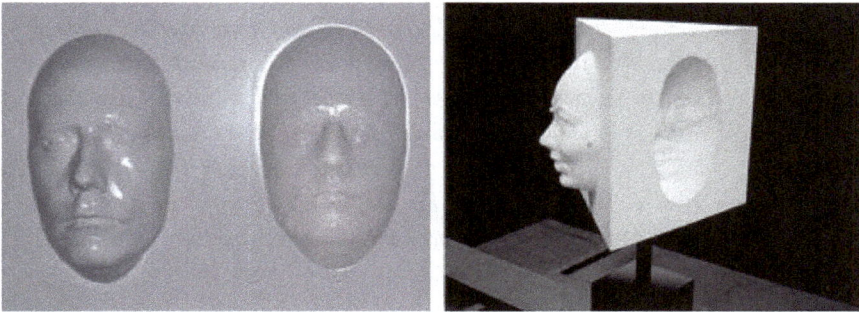

In both pictures, the image on the left is in normal relief, while the image on the right is concave. For most people, the brain finds a concave image of the human face unacceptable and makes a natural correction in line with our experience and learnt perception of what we know about a real face. Even when we know something is one way, we can still have the deep-rooted belief that it is another way. We are so used to interpreting reality in familiar ways, that it's hard for the mind to conceive of something different to its learnt expectations.

I'm sure many of you will have seen the next illusions. We know that they are flat drawings on the ground, but our mind insists they have structure and depth.

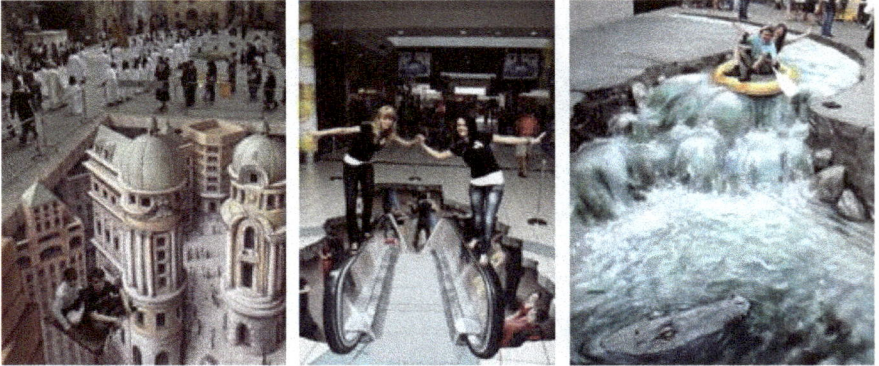

"Now, you each generally agree, I am sure, that you sit upon a couch. You do not perceive the same couch. You only perceive your own idea constructions. You cannot perceive those of another. Telepathically you transpose your ideas in line with what you know of the other person's thinking. You agree that the couch is here. Now, it is true that within your physical system [...] you can measure your couch. I expect at any moment anyone will get a ruler and measure it and then say to me that the couch is so long – how can you say it is not one couch? However, within your physical system the instruments themselves are distorted and, of course, they will agree with what they measure. There is no reason why they should not. Telepathically you all agree upon the placement of objects and their dimensions."[47]

The Higgs Boson

At the time of originally writing this book, the search was continuing for the illusive Higgs Boson – sometimes referred to as 'The God Particle' because it's said to be what caused the "Big Bang" that created our universe many years ago. Essentially, scientists were telling us that the Higgs Boson could unify everything in the universe and close the gaps of mystery relating to the positions and actions of other already known particles and their properties. By the end of 2011, the researchers at CERN (Franco–Swiss border) with their LEP (Large Electron Positron) Collider had narrowed the area of the Higgs to be between 114 Gev (giga–electron volts) and 145 Gev.

---

[47] Seth, The Early Class Sessions 2, ESP Class Session, June 23, 1970

This soon narrowed to between 115 Gev and 127 Gev with additional results from America's Fermilab and their Tevatron collider but, with both the CERN LHC[48], CMS[49] and ATLAS[50] teams working on resolving the project, by January 2012 the gap had closed to between 124 Gev and 126 Gev – at the lower end of the scale of potential masses.[51]

On 4 July, 2012, scientists announced the observation of the Higgs boson, the elusive particle that gives almost all other particles their mass – and thus lays the foundation for the matter that forms us and everything we see around us in the universe. The news thrilled the world and made international headlines.

To Summarise

- At some level of creation, everything knows what it is
- Creative mind allows sentient beings to be co-creators
- Beliefs form to give individual and collective views of personal reality
- Accumulations of commonality develop into QMS
- Collective perception of similar reality solidifies into "truths"
- It is difficult to change established solidifications – but, not impossible
- The planet Earth is our most enduring QMS and its solidity was formed over a very long time period in order to achieve stability for the safety and well-being of evolving sentient beings

---

[48] Large Hadron Collider
[49] Compact Muon Spectrometer
[50] Argonne Tandem Linear Accelerator System
[51] This isn't too surprising as lower vibrational energy is usually associated with greater mass and if we are getting close to consciousness, this would be among the highest of vibrational energy.

- Science continues to apply tests to physical reality and will continue to make many discoveries. However, without an acknowledgement of a non-physical, intelligent consciousness, science will never fully understand how the universe was not only created, but continues to be created on both an individual and collective scale.

As mentioned earlier, I hold a speculative opinion that perhaps it is no coincidence that past civilisations chose to leave messages in stone in preference to any other material, because the QMS of stone is long established and unlikely to decay before successive generations have had chance to experience it in their realities.

Consciousness and Time

"When man began to experiment with memory, there were innumerable instances where the emerging ego consciousness did not distinguish clearly enough between the past and the present. The past in the present would appear so brilliantly that man could not react adequately in circumstances of time that he had himself created. The future was blocked, practically speaking, to preserve freedom of action and so encourage physical exploration, curiosity, and creativity. With memory, however, mental projections into the future were of course also possible so that man could plan his activities in time, and force probable events. "Ghost images" of the future probabilities always acted as mental stimuli for physical explorations in all areas, and of all kinds. These ghost images provided stimuli for mental, spiritual, and physical experience."[52]

The Spacious Present

Seth[53] often talks about our individual experience existing in what he calls "the spacious present." It's a simultaneous existence of everything, accessed from what he refers to as our "moment point." Originally, I thought the moment point was every moment of my

---

[52] Seth: The "Unknown" Reality, Volume 1. Jane Roberts Session 686 February 27, 1974.
[53] Op.Cit. Seth

now but, collectively, a moment point can be a whole era or lifetime. It can indeed be the whole existence of our understanding of the Earth. Furthermore, since we experience physical reality, with linear time and a sense of past, present, and future, this cannot exist in a universe where everything is simultaneous and there is no real time or separate intervals of experience. The only way our physical reality can exist, to my mind, is if we are in a cosmic bubble of reality. Perhaps this bubble is also a non-physical psychological reality, and certainly way beyond our comprehension to understand.

Finally...

The quantum mass superstructures of science and spirituality are now colliding touch planes. The changes that we all perceive as a human race on a rock in space, are quickening in pace. Our global awareness and witness to so many events and discoveries is greater than it has ever been in the Earth's history. In a space of only about 30 years, we went from mechanical typewrites and landline telephones to computers and 'smart' phones. Prior to this, my own grandmother witnessed the advent of automobiles and died at 100, having also seen rockets to the Moon and the advent of computers. Everything in our perception is speeding up. The rates of planetary vibrational frequency are also increasing – drawing us into a new level of consciousness and awareness.

Everything has its place – it's just that we thought that some of those places were more fixed than we now begin to realise.

Always consider the possibility of that which exists, but cannot be seen, or that which is seen, but does not exist – at least in the form that you perceive.

Do not dismiss the absurdity of a suggestion as naïve or irrelevant to your own belief or research – for everyone and everything holds a part of the answer that you need to advance. An absurd comment, or a book like this one you have been reading, could trigger a thought in you that leads to a new discovery.

Also consider that most of us like to believe in the possible, but often, in psychological make-up, know, from listening to others, that those same things are impossible – at least until new discoveries are made and something changes our perception.

Working in a world where we can live in, and experience, a physical sense of reality is quite amazing. Living in a world made up of QMS is also amazing – but sometimes, also quite scary.
I shall leave you with this, from Seth:

"Ideas have an electromagnetic reality. Beliefs are strong ideas about the nature of reality. Ideas generate emotion. Like attracts like, so similar ideas group about each other and you accept those that fit in with your particular "system" of ideas.

"Limiting ideas therefore predispose you to accept others of a similar nature. Exuberant ideas of freedom, spontaneity and joy automatically collect others of their kind also. There is a constant interplay between yourself and others in the exchange of ideas, both telepathically and on a conscious level."[54]

---

[54] Seth, The Nature of Personal Reality, Chapter 3, Session 616, September 20, 1972

Other information by Richard Gentle, and a link to the current Starlab:

Websites:

keekoo.co.uk

richardgentle.com

https://www.starlab.es (Starlab in Barcelona)

Social Media:

facebook.com/GentleAnswers

Appreciation:

paypal.me/RichardGentle

www.ingramcontent.com/pod-product-compliance
Lightning Source LLC
Chambersburg PA
CBHW071637040426
42452CB00009B/1667